SCRAPPY QUILTS

COLORING BOOK

JOAN FORD

A SCRAPTHERAPY® BOOK

The Taunton Press

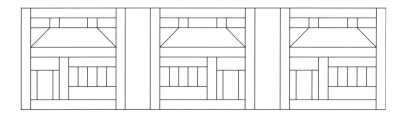

The Taunton Press, Inc.
63 South Main Street
PO Box 5506
Newtown, CT 06470-5506

Email: tp@taunton.com

Illustrator: Joan Ford

ISBN: 978-1-63186-706-4

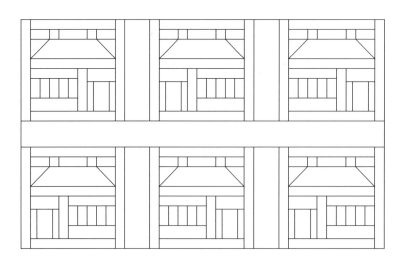

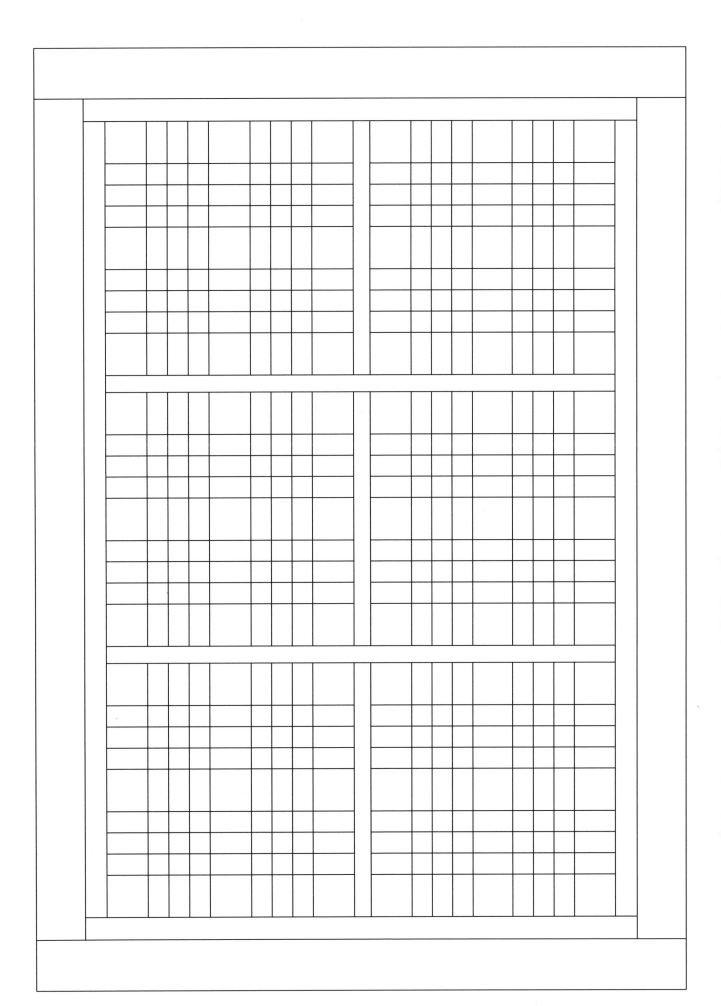

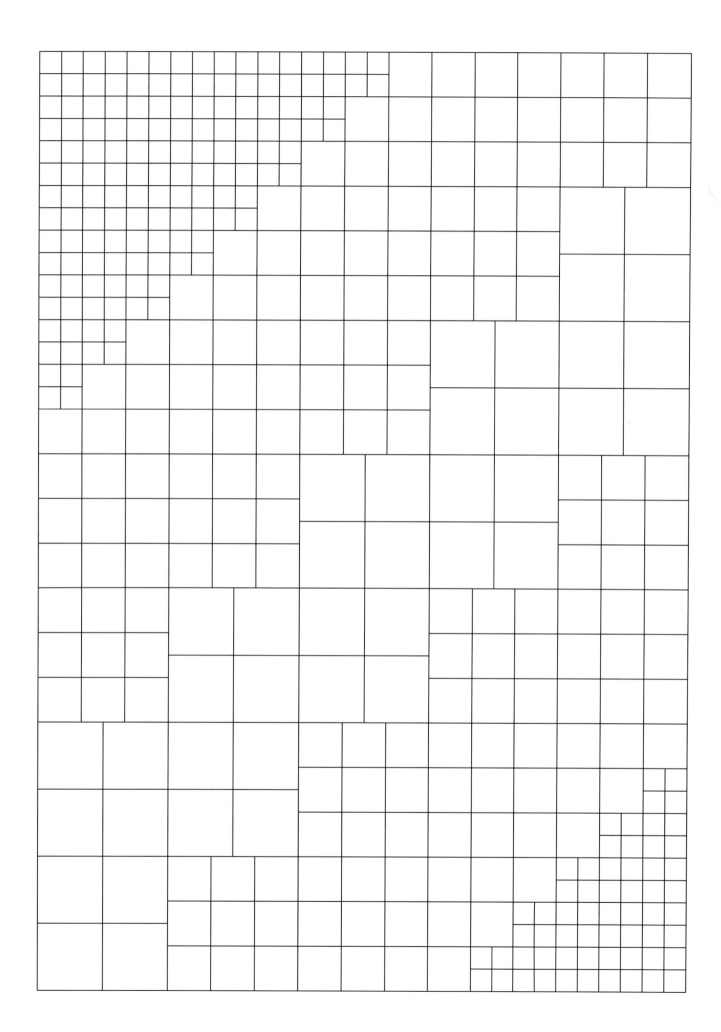

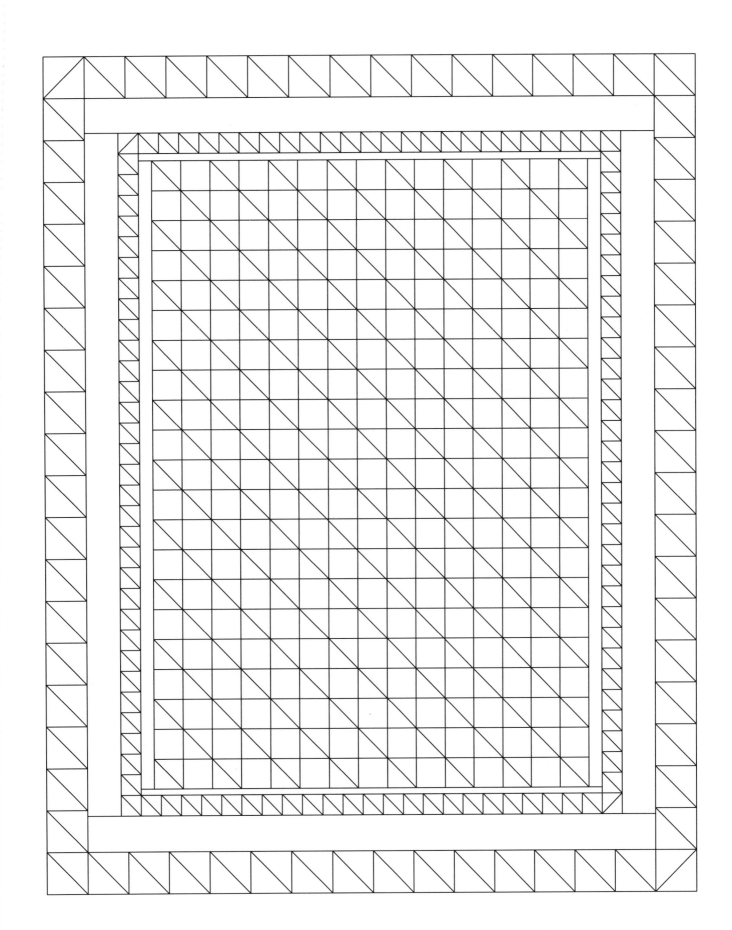

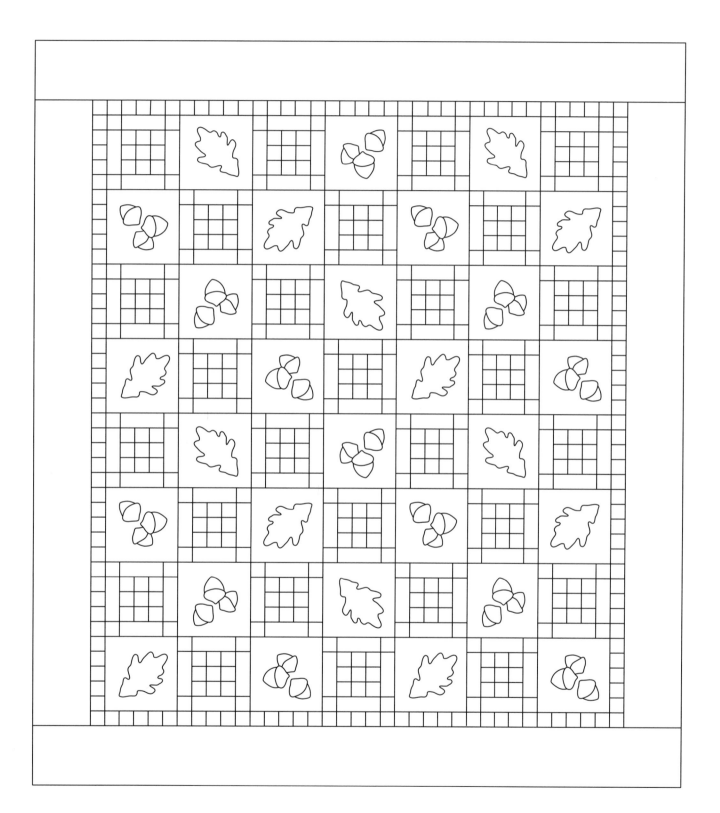

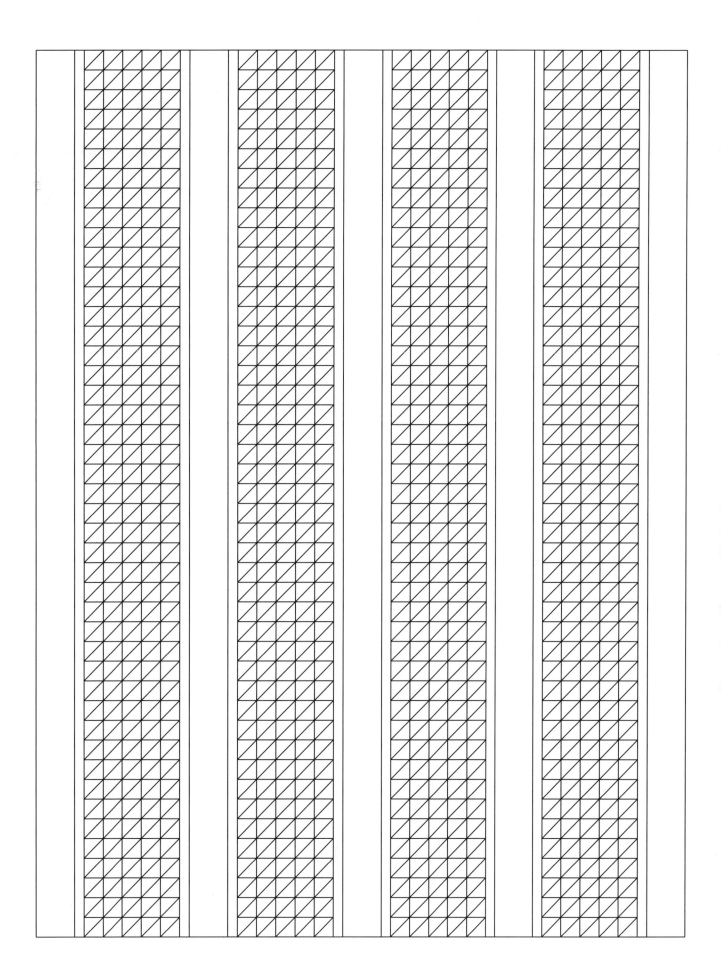

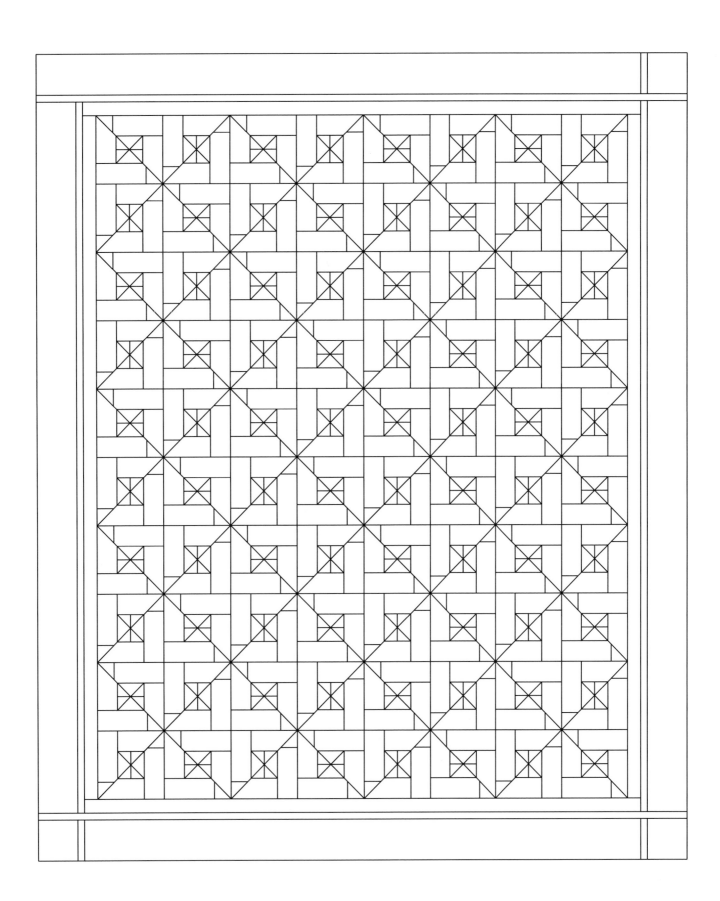

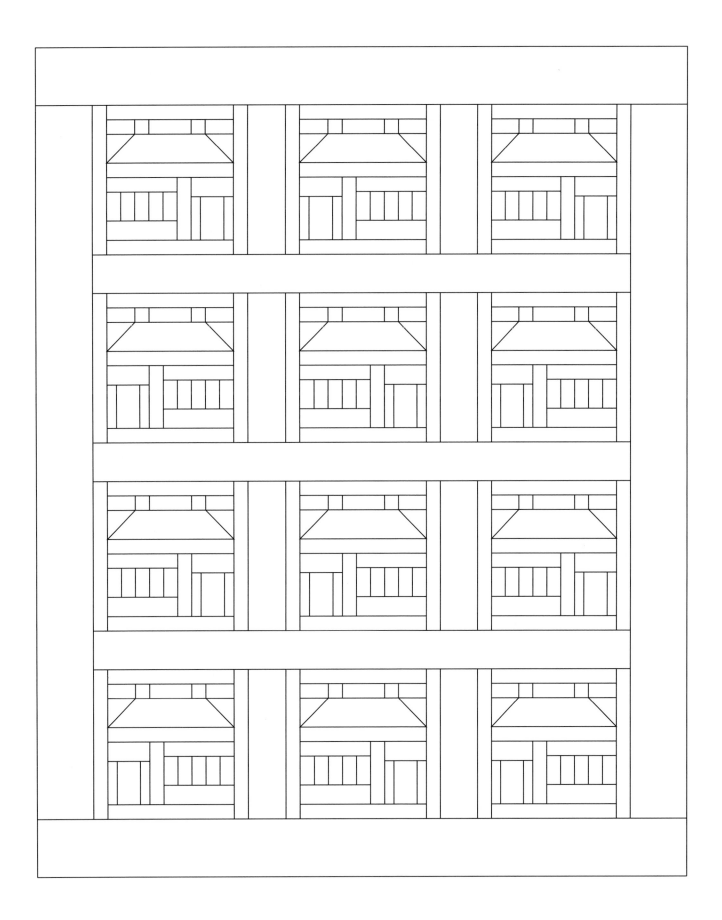

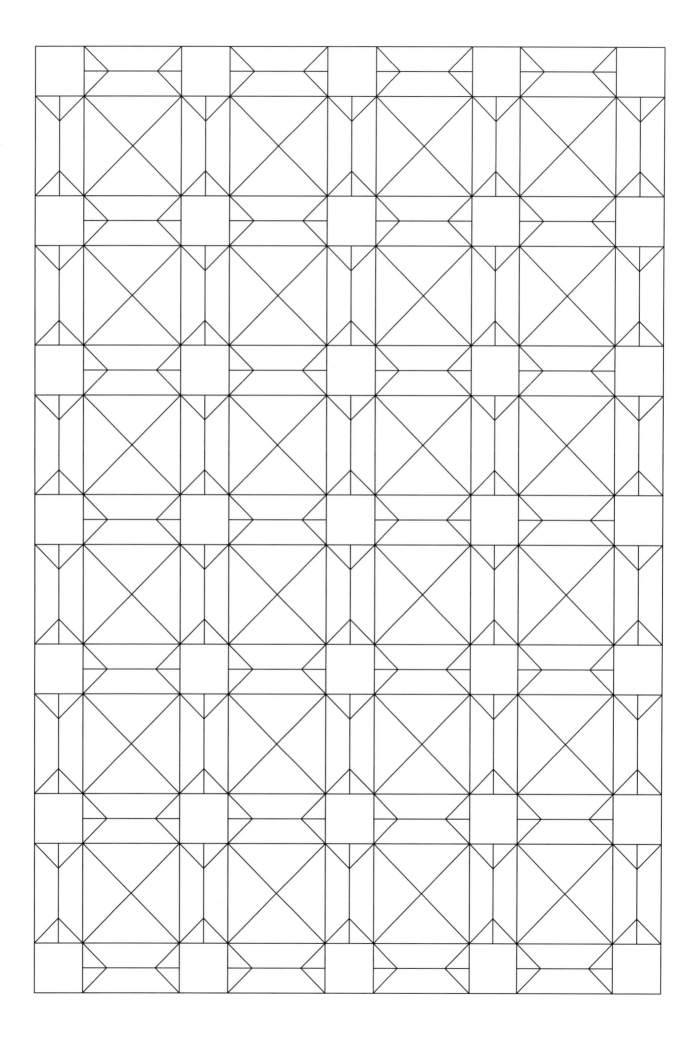

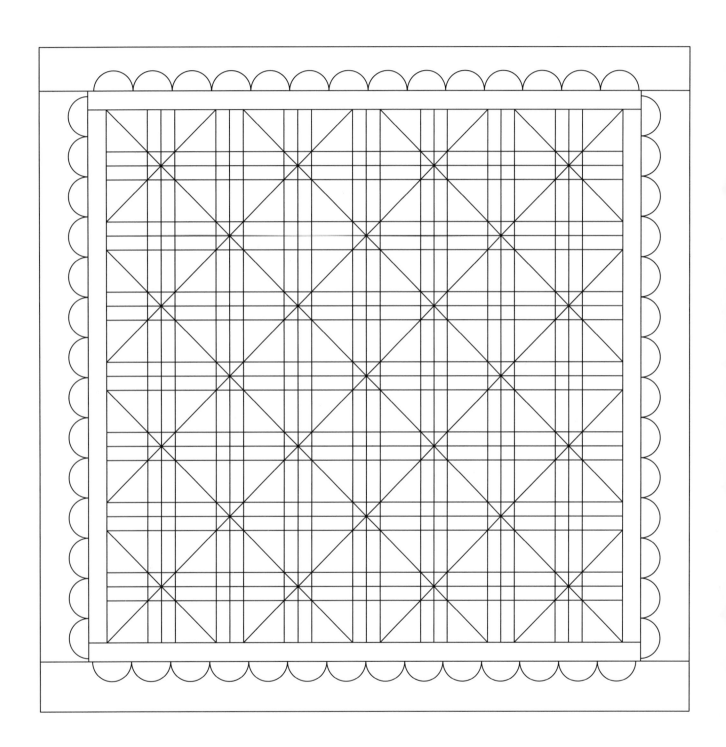

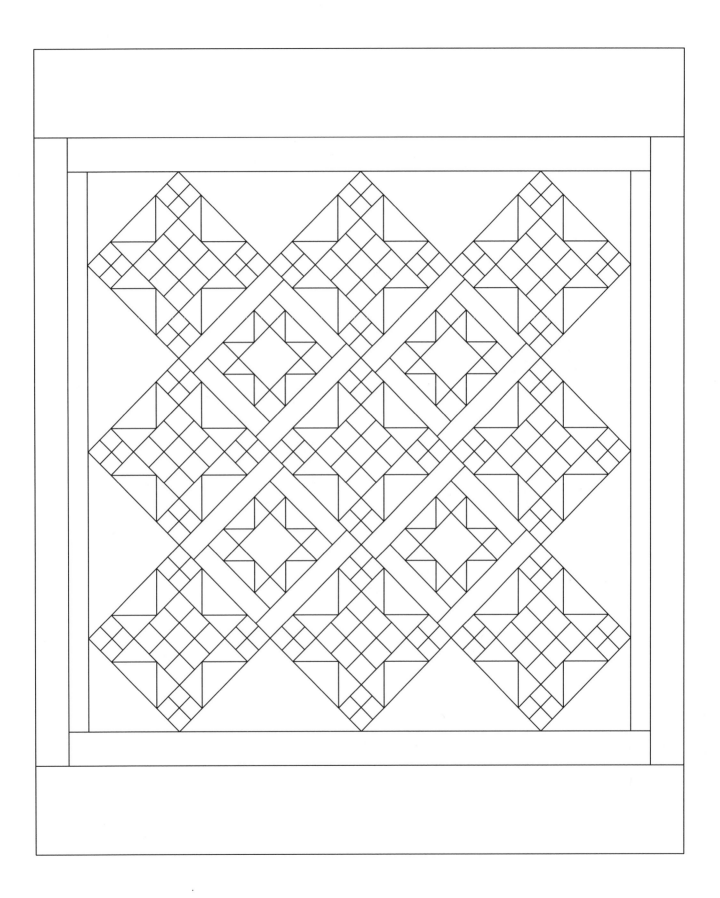

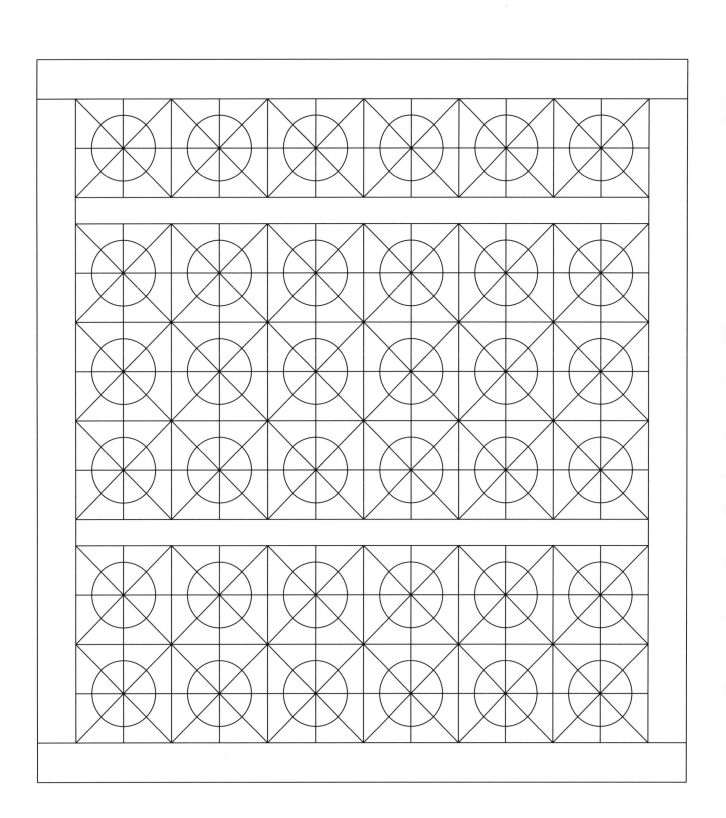

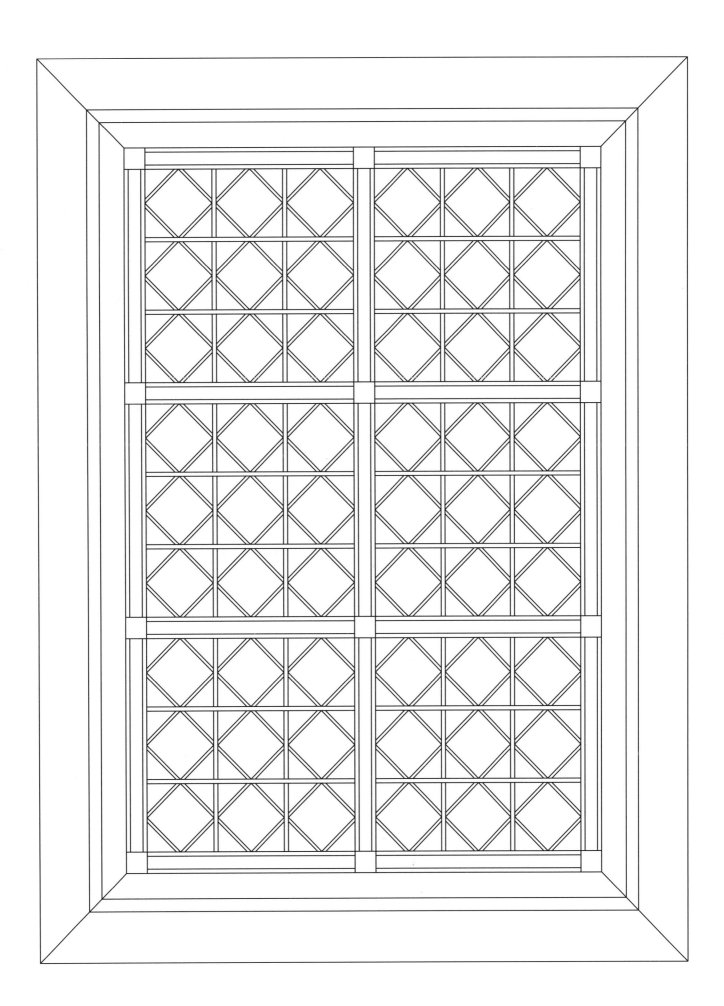

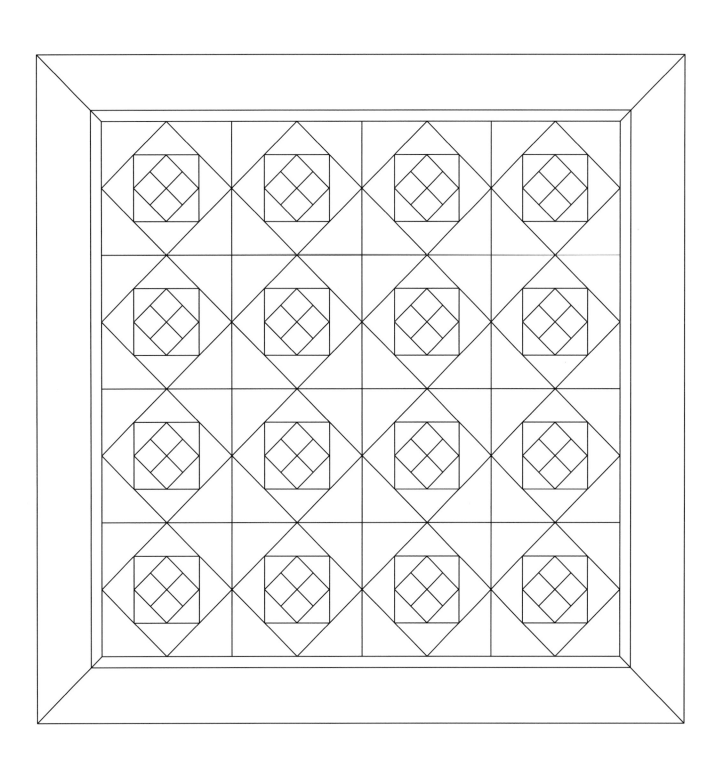

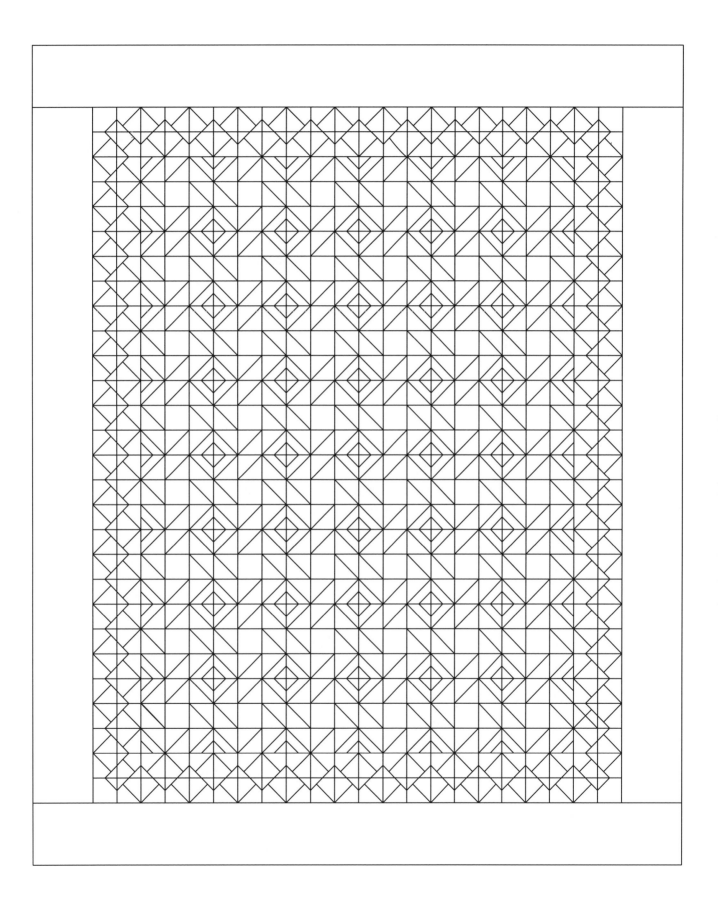

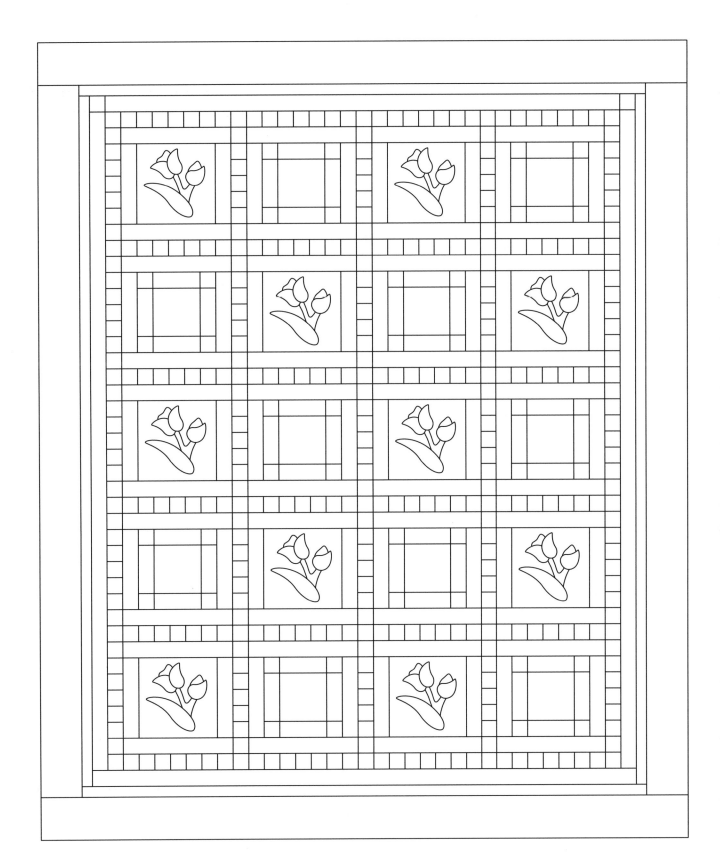

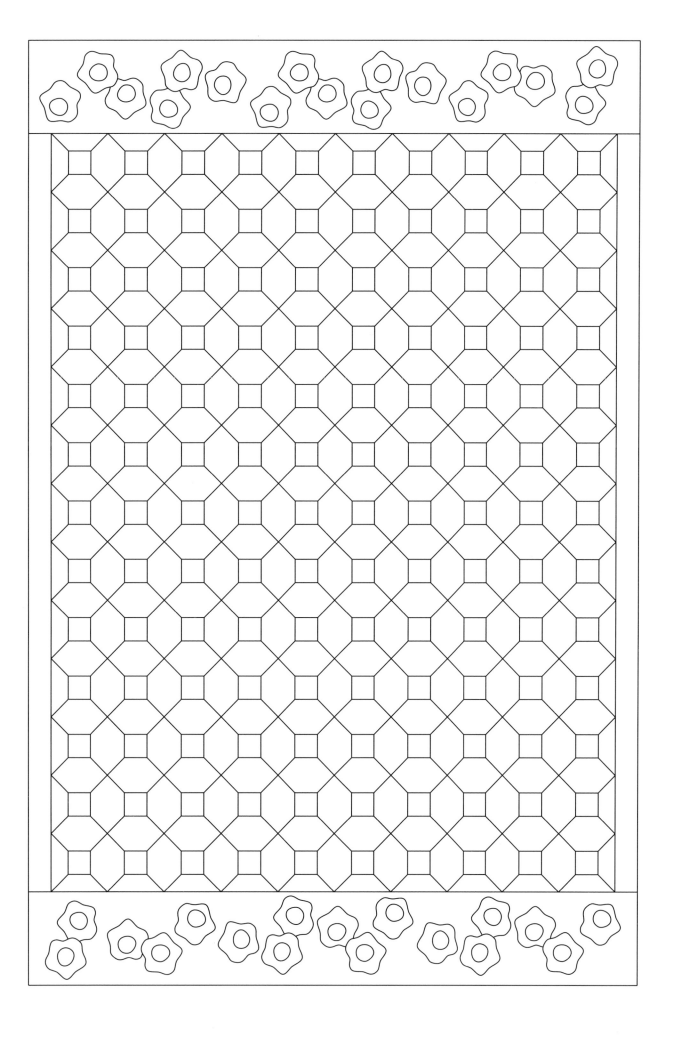